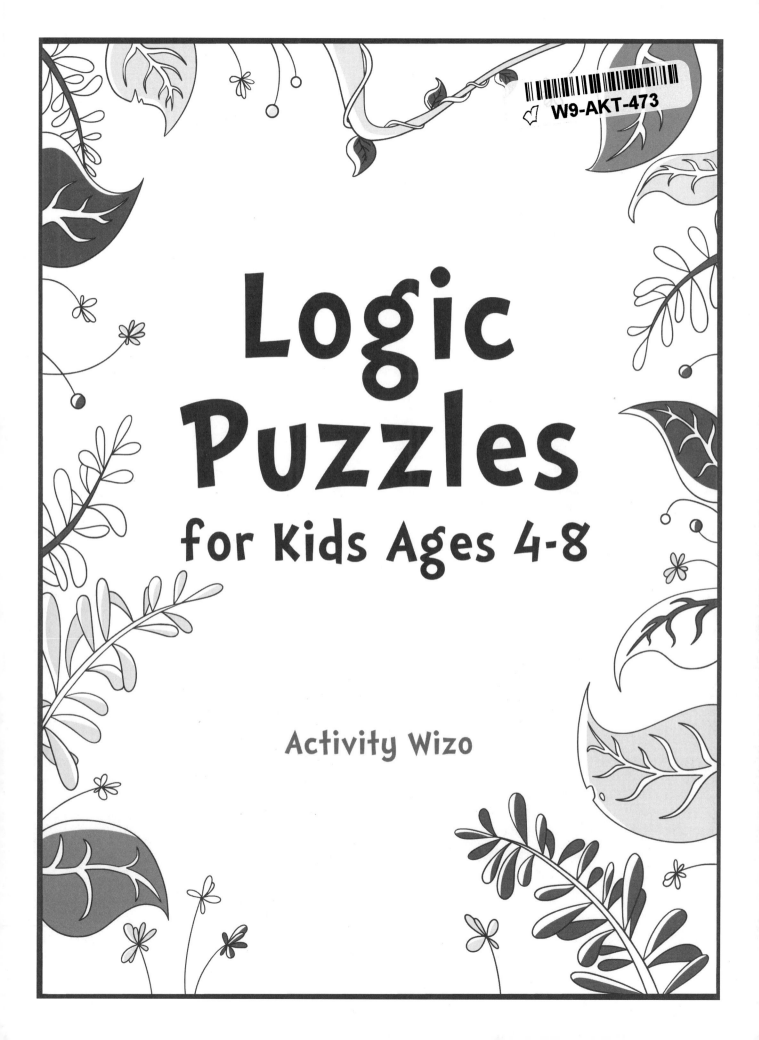

Logic
Puzzles
for Kids Ages 4-8

Activity Wizo

Please consider writing a review!
Just visit: activitywizo.com/review

Have questions? We want to hear from you!
Email us at: support@activitywizo.com

ISBN: 978-1-951806-33-0

FREE BONUS

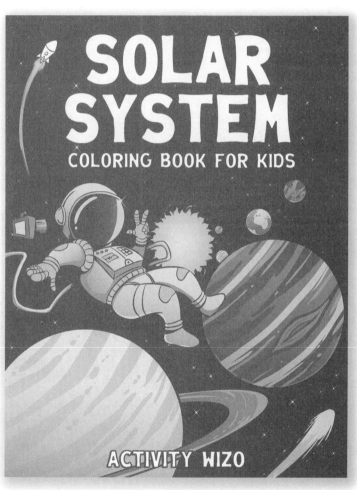

Just visit:
activitywizo.com/free

Table of Contents

Chapter 1
Jungle Fever

Mining Carts

Write the missing numbers inside the carts.

Row 1: ☐ 2 3 ☐ ☐ 6 ☐ 8

Row 2: 9 10 ☐ ☐ 13 ☐ 15 ☐

Row 3: 10 9 ☐ 7 ☐ ☐ 4 3

Row 4: 16 15 ☐ ☐ 12 ☐ 10 9

Row 5: 2 4 ☐ 8 10 ☐ ☐ 16

Jungle Birds

Count the number of each kind of bird and write it down.

Missing Gear

Draw a line to connect the kids to their missing gear.

Mason	Mia	Emma	Liam	Ethan

Jungle Kids

Circle the jungle kid that comes next based on the pattern.

Mushrooms

Draw the correct number of mushrooms based on the pattern from top to bottom.

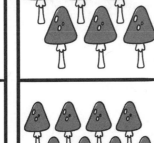

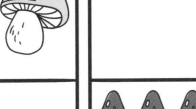

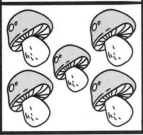

8

Explorer Equipment

Circle the equipment that each kid needs.

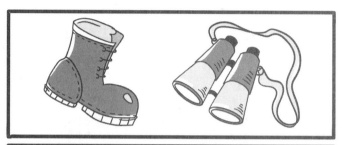 is to

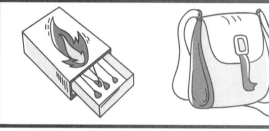 is to

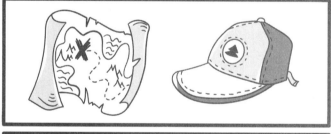 is to

 is to

 is to

9

Forest Fun

Draw an object to add for each group.

Jungle Animals

Draw an X on top of the animal that does not belong.

11

Tree Houses

Read the clues and draw a line from the kids to the correct tree houses.

Ethan's house has 2 square windows.
Mason's house has 1 circle window.
Liam's house has a flower pot by the window.
Emma's house has a door with a heart.

Emma   Ethan   Mia   Liam   Mason

Chapter 2
Space Walk

Constellations

Draw a line from dot to dot in order.

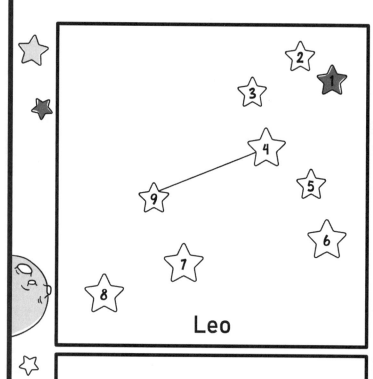

Leo

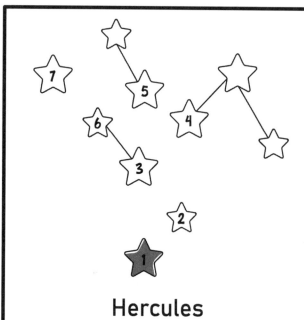

Hercules

Little Bear

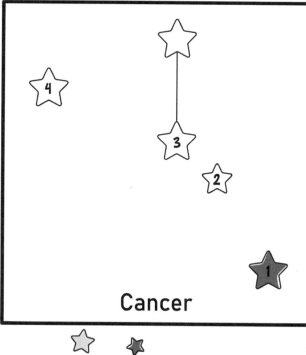

Cancer

15

Space Walk

Comet Trail

Color the picture according to numbers.

| 1 | Brown | 2 | Red | 3 | Orange | 4 | Yellow |

16

Space Stuff

Space Walk

Mark an X over the objects that don't belong in space.

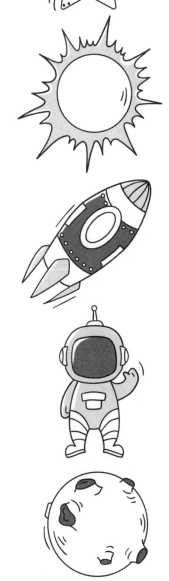

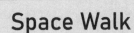

Solar System

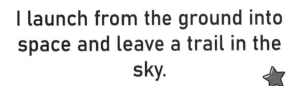

Draw a line to connect the object to the correct description.

I launch from the ground into space and leave a trail in the sky.

I go into space using my space suit and riding a large rocket.

You can see me at night, sometimes full, sometimes half, at other times only a crescent.

In daylight you can see me, but don't look straight at me.

I'm a tiny little speck in the night sky.

18

Moon Rocks

Draw the moon based on the pattern.

19

Space Junk

Draw the correct object based on the pattern.

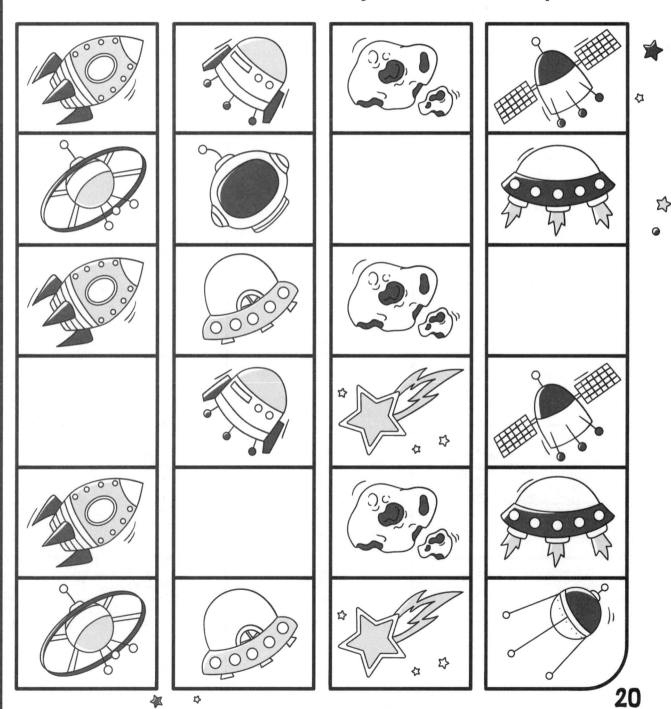

20

Satellite Link

Draw a line to link the correct satellites.

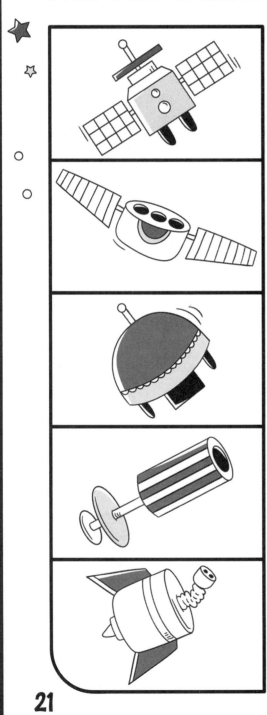

21

Cosmic Rhymes

Draw a line from the words to the space objects that rhyme.

Car

Lantern

Spoon

One

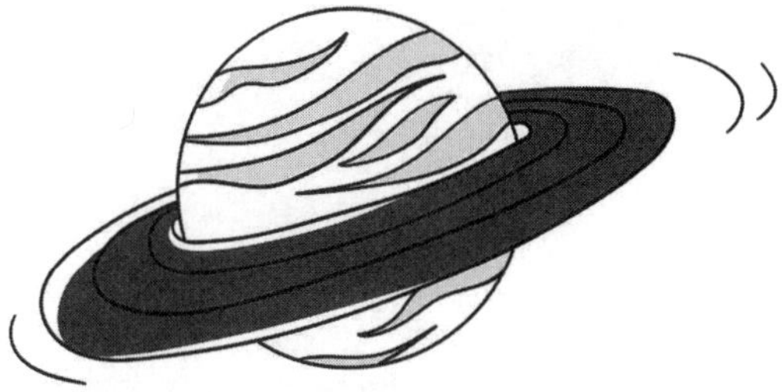

Pocket

Star Shine

Color the stars according to the clues.

The left-most star shines blue.
The right-most star radiates red.
The star in the middle shines yellow.
The biggest star is color purple.
The smallest star is color green.
The star with the least amount of rays is color orange.
The star with the most amount of rays is color pink.

Which in Space

Answer each question and circle the correct object.

Which object can be seen during the day, but you can't look at it because it can damage your eyes?

Which object can be seen at night and has different phases?

Which object can fly up in the sky and into space?

Which object can shine brightly in the night sky even if it's very small?

24

Chapter 3
City Escape

Cause and Effect

Circle the event on the right which shows what would happen next.

Let's Build

Write the numbers 1 to 5 to show the steps in building a house.

28

Pool Party

Compare the two pictures and circle the differences in the picture on the right.

29

Time in the City

Circle the correct answer according to the time of day.

Morning / Afternoon / Night

Morning / Afternoon / Night

Morning / Afternoon / Night

Morning / Afternoon / Night

What in the City

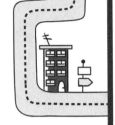

Draw a line connecting the object to the correct description.

I'm round and I bounce around the ground.

I have many wheels and windows, and I bring you from home to school and back.

I only have two wheels but I'm fun to ride and I have a bell.

I can carry lots of water for you, but you will have to pick me up.

I have 3 hands and 12 numbers and I tell the time.

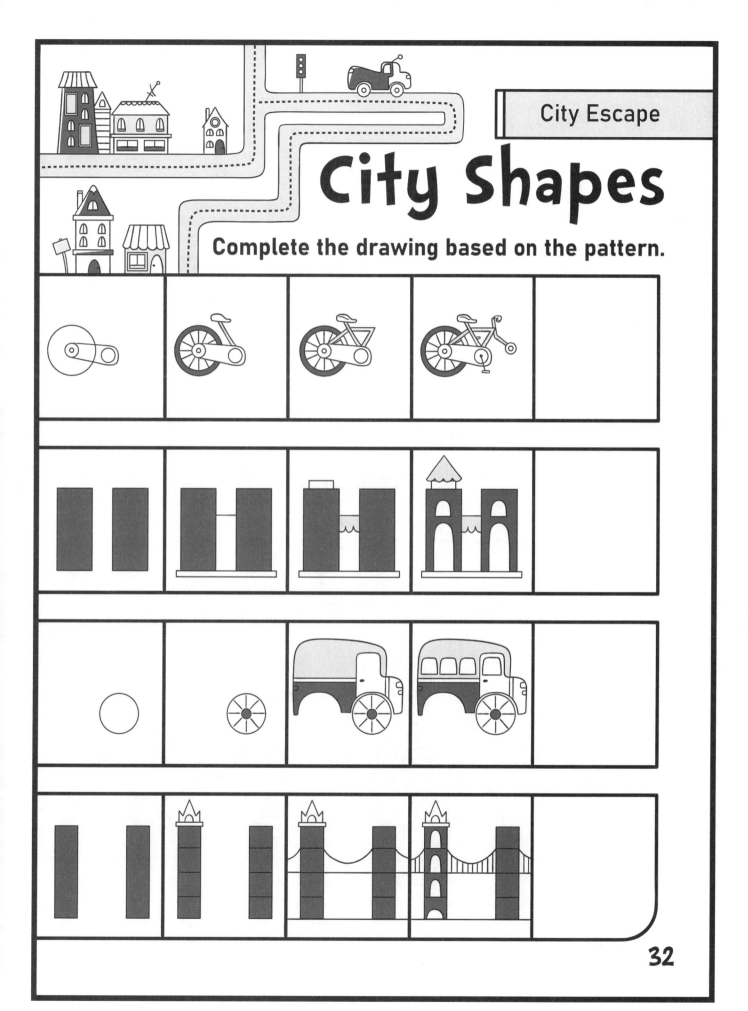

City Shapes

Complete the drawing based on the pattern.

32

City's Edge

Count the number of edges on each object and write the nubmer inside the box.

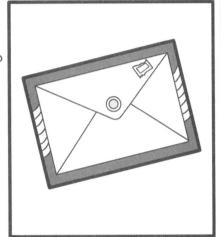

☐ ☐ ☐

☐ ☐ ☐

Triangle Town

Find and circle all 5 triangle-shaped objects hidden in the picture.

34

City Sports

Draw a line to connect the sport to the correct kid.

Emma   Ethan   Mia   Liam   Mason

Shapes and Colors

Color the shapes according to the instructions.

The square is color blue.
Color the circle green.
Beside the green circle is a brown triangle.
At one corner, there is a yellow star.
In the middle is a red heart.

D
A
B
C

B
A
C

Chapter 4

Pirate Plunder

Size Matters

Write the numbers 1 to 5 according to the sizes of the objects from smallest to biggest.

Edge of the Ocean

Draw a circle around the bigger object in each comparison.

Under the Sea

Draw a line connecting the animal to the correct description.

I'm a horse, but not the kind that gallops on land.

I have many arms, as many as 8, and I spray ink to get away.

I have 5 arms and shaped like a star, but I'm underwater and not up in the sky.

I have sharp teeth, lots of them. I'm big and I swim fast.

I'm a bird that loves to swim, that's because I can't really fly.

Which of Which

Answer each question and circle the correct object.

Which object is made of glass and can break apart when dropped on the floor?

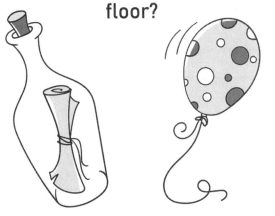

Which animal lives in the ocean, has pincers, and walks sideways?

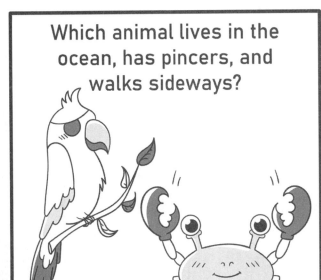

Which object is made of wood and contains treasure?

Which object has a short fuse and can explode?

42

What is Next

Draw the correct object based on the pattern.

Shapes at Sea

Circle the shape that has the correct number of sides.

4

5

0

10

8

 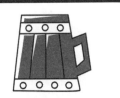

14

12

9

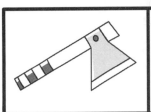 

Pirate Sounds

Draw a line to connect the rhyming objects.

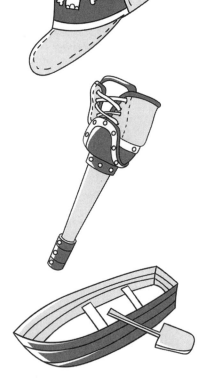

Soda Bottles

Find and circle all 10 soda bottles hidden in the picture.

Pirate Plunder

Oceaneering

Draw an X over the animal or object that does not belong.

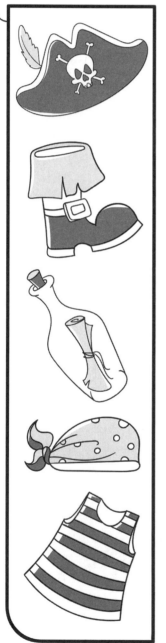

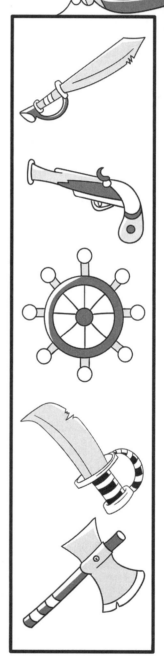

47

Pirate Kids

Read the clues. Draw a line to connect the kid to the correct object.

Ethan loves animals and enjoys the company of pets.
Liam enjoys playing pirate.
Emma loves to see far away places.
Mia likes to dig for treasure.

Emma   Ethan   Mia   Liam   Mason

48

Chapter 5
Jurassic Trip

Dino Drawings

Write the numbers 1–4 to show the order of each drawing.

51

Let's Dig

Circle 5 objects that you will need to dig up fossils.

Kids in the Dino Park

Compare the two pictures and circle the differences in the bottom picture.

53

Feelings and Dinos

Draw a line to connect the image to the feeling.

Happy

Sad

Angry

Scared

Surprised

54

Dinosaur Patterns

Draw the correct object based on the pattern.

Dino Catching

Circle all the dinosaurs in the scene.

Shadow Hunting

Draw a line to connect the shadow to their dinosaur.

57

Animals Out

Mark an X over the animals that are not dinosaurs.

Dino Facts

Draw a line from the dinosaur to the correct sentence.

A dinosaur with 3 horns and a large frill.

One of the most fearsome dinosaurs ever.

A small but fast carnivorous dinosaur.

A dinosaur with lots of back plates and a long tail.

A very large flying dinosaur with a long beak.

Building the Zoo

Draw a line from the sentence to the tool it's describing.

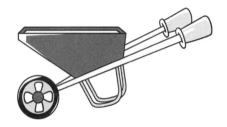

A tool used to hammer
a nail into wood.

Something you can use
to dig up dirt.

This tool can be used to
cut wood in half.

You can carry dirt from
one place to another.

You can pull out nails
with this tool.

Chapter 6
Farming Fun

Farm Shadows

Draw a line to connect the shadow to their farm animal.

63

Wild Animals

Mark an X over the 10 animals that are not farm animals.

Into the Barn

Draw a line connecting the animal to the correct description.

I have 4 legs and can run fast. I neigh and gallop with my other animal friends.

I'm usually pink in color and I produce a lot of bacon.

I wake up early in the morning to make some noise and wake other people up.

Baaah I say. I have thick white wool to make clothes for people.

I'm colored black and white and I produce milk.

Farm Stuff

Answer each question and circle the correct object.

Which building is made of wood and can store a lot of hay?

Which is the tall cylindrical building which can store a lot of grain?

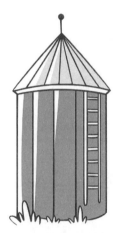

Which is a small building where chickens live?

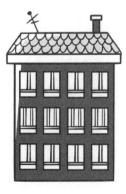

Which is a small building where tools are kept?

Chicken Dance

Draw the correct chicken based on the pattern.

Horse Run

Draw the correct horse based on the pattern.

Farming Fun

Link the Fences

Draw a line to link the correct fences.

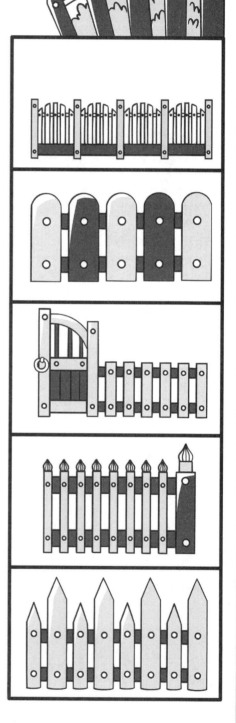

69

Farm Facts

Draw a line from the animal to the correct sentence.

An animal that can lay eggs. The young ones are called chicks.

A vehicle that can help farmers till the soil in a farm land.

A large wooden building that can store hay and house animals.

A building that has 4 blades that rotate to mill grains.

An animal that can produce milk. It has big black spots on it's body.

Farm Kids

Read the clues. Draw a line to connect the kid to the correct object.

Ethan loves small four-legged farm animals.
Liam enjoys riding a horse.
Emma loves to collect chicken eggs.
Mia likes to gather milk.

Emma	Ethan	Mia	Liam	Mason

71

Farm Animals

Draw an X on top of the animal that does not belong.

72

Answer Key

3 Mining Carts
Correct numbers:

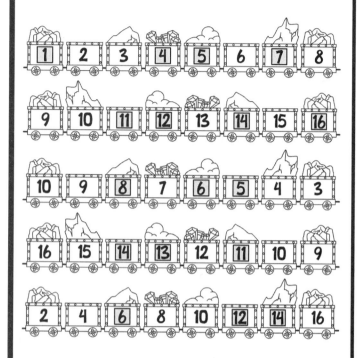

4 Fruit Snacks

5 Jungle Birds
Correct numbers:

6 Missing Gear

Mason   Mia   Emma   Liam   Ethan

75

7 Jungle Kids

8 Mushrooms

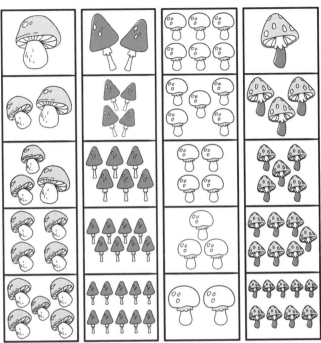

9 Explorer Equipment

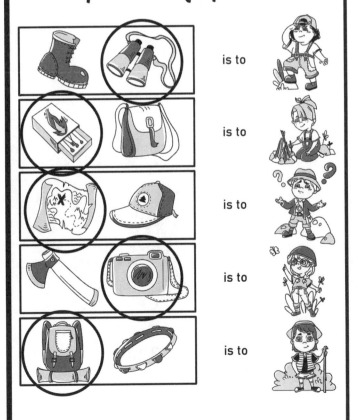

is to

is to

is to

is to

is to

10 Forest Fun

11 Jungle Animals

12 Tree Houses

Emma　Ethan　Mia　Liam　Mason

15 Constellations

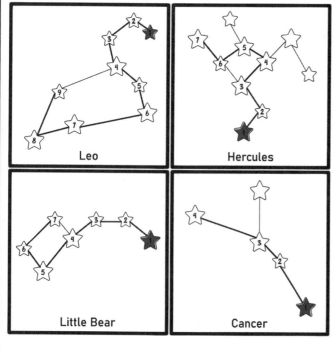

Leo

Hercules

Little Bear

Cancer

16 Comet Trail

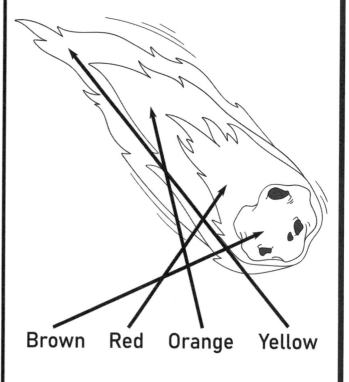

Brown　Red　Orange　Yellow

17 Space Stuff

18 Solar System

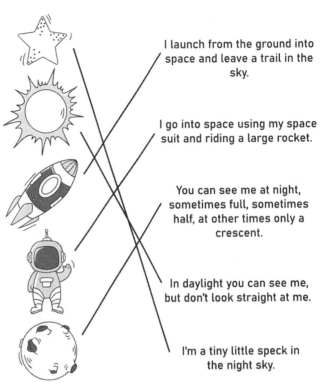

I launch from the ground into space and leave a trail in the sky.

I go into space using my space suit and riding a large rocket.

You can see me at night, sometimes full, sometimes half, at other times only a crescent.

In daylight you can see me, but don't look straight at me.

I'm a tiny little speck in the night sky.

19 Moon Rocks

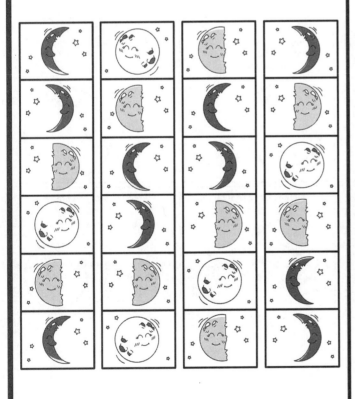

20 Space Junk

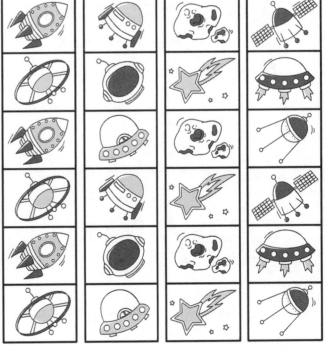

21 Satellite Link

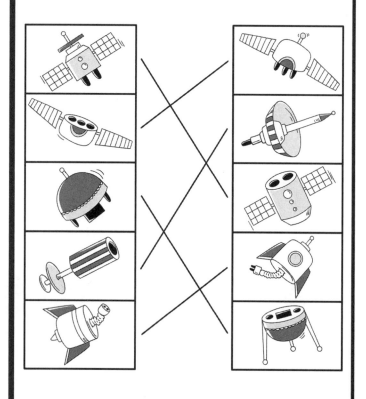

22 Cosmic Rhymes

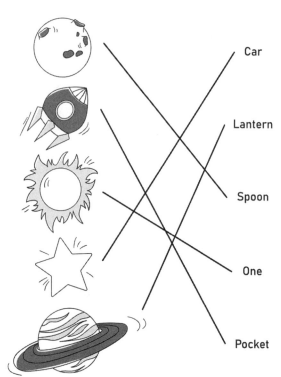

Car

Lantern

Spoon

One

Pocket

23 Star Shine

Blue   Purple   Orange

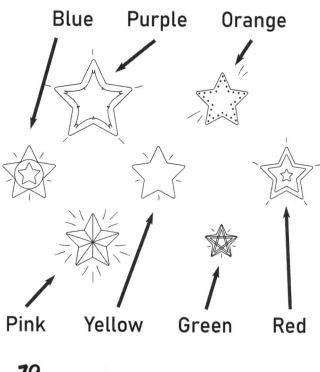

Pink   Yellow   Green   Red

24 Which in Space

Which object can be seen during the day, but you can't look at it because it can damage your eyes?

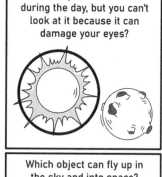

Which object can be seen at night and has different phases?

Which object can fly up in the sky and into space?

Which object can shine brightly in the night sky even if it's very small?

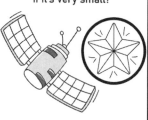

27 Cause and Effect

28 Let's Build

Correct order :

1	3	2	4	5
4	1	3	2	5
3	4	2	5	1
1	3	5	2	4

29 Pool Party

Differences :

30 Time in the City

Morning / Afternoon / Night

Morning / Afternoon / Night

Morning / Afternoon / Night

Morning / Afternoon / Night

80

31 What in the City

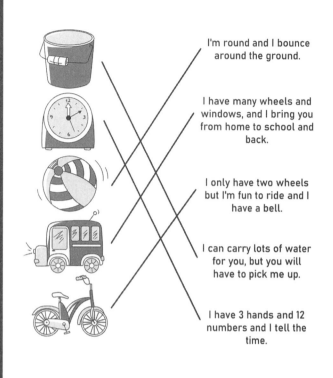

I'm round and I bounce around the ground.

I have many wheels and windows, and I bring you from home to school and back.

I only have two wheels but I'm fun to ride and I have a bell.

I can carry lots of water for you, but you will have to pick me up.

I have 3 hands and 12 numbers and I tell the time.

32 City Shapes

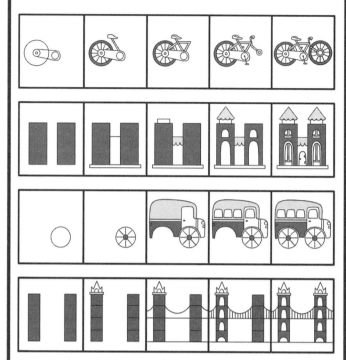

33 City's Edge
Correct numbers:

34 Triangle Town

35 City Sports

36 Shapes and Colors

39 Size Matters

Correct order :

40 Edge of the Ocean

82

41 Under the Sea

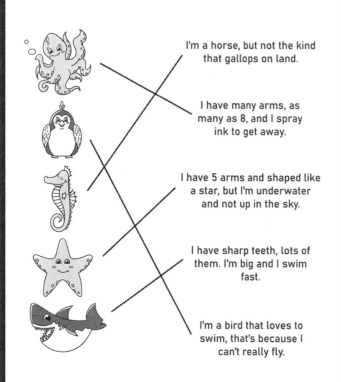

I'm a horse, but not the kind that gallops on land.

I have many arms, as many as 8, and I spray ink to get away.

I have 5 arms and shaped like a star, but I'm underwater and not up in the sky.

I have sharp teeth, lots of them. I'm big and I swim fast.

I'm a bird that loves to swim, that's because I can't really fly.

42 Which of Which

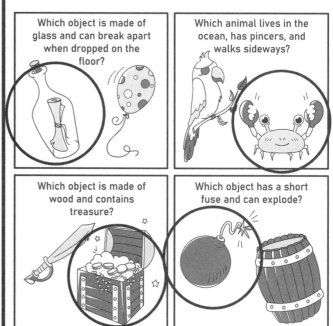

Which object is made of glass and can break apart when dropped on the floor?

Which animal lives in the ocean, has pincers, and walks sideways?

Which object is made of wood and contains treasure?

Which object has a short fuse and can explode?

43 What is Next

44 Shapes at Sea

45 Pirate Sounds

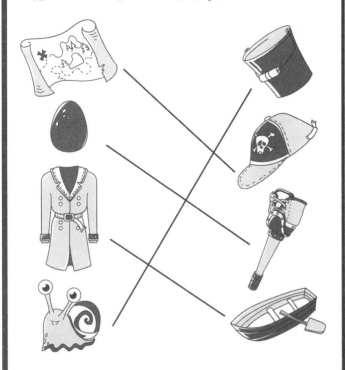

46 Soda Bottles

47 Oceaneering

48 Pirate Kids

Emma   Ethan   Mia   Liam   Mason

84

51 Dino Drawings

Correct order :

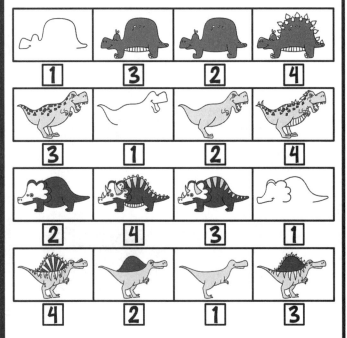

52 Let's Dig

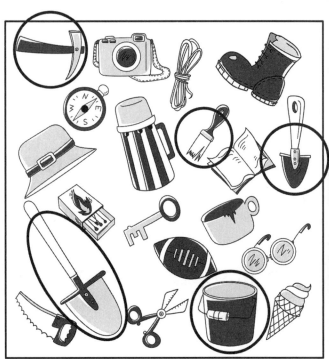

53 Kids in the Dino Park

Differences :

54 Feelings and Dinos

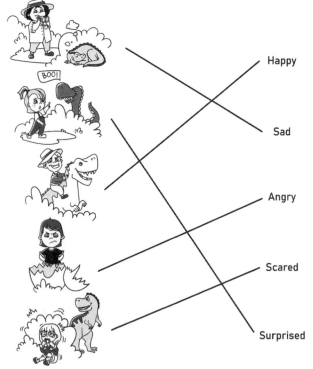

Happy

Sad

Angry

Scared

Surprised

55 Dinosaur Patterns

56 Dino Catching

57 Shadow Hunting

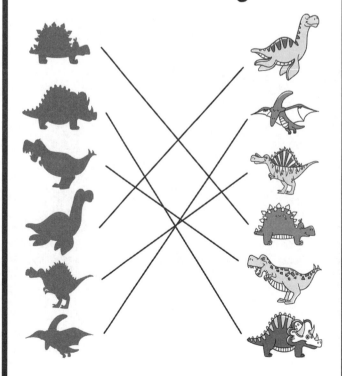

58 Animals Out

59 Dino Facts

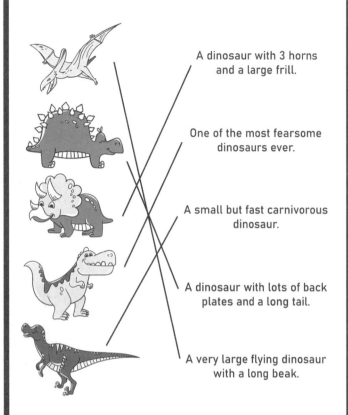

A dinosaur with 3 horns and a large frill.

One of the most fearsome dinosaurs ever.

A small but fast carnivorous dinosaur.

A dinosaur with lots of back plates and a long tail.

A very large flying dinosaur with a long beak.

60 Building the Zoo

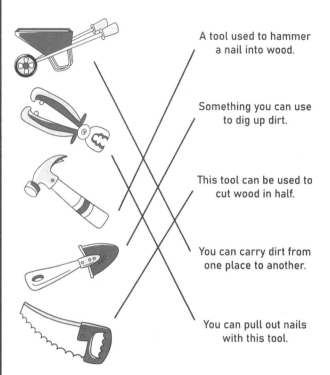

A tool used to hammer a nail into wood.

Something you can use to dig up dirt.

This tool can be used to cut wood in half.

You can carry dirt from one place to another.

You can pull out nails with this tool.

63 Farm Shadows

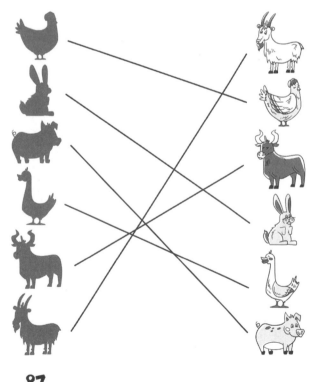

64 Wild Animals

65 Into the Barn

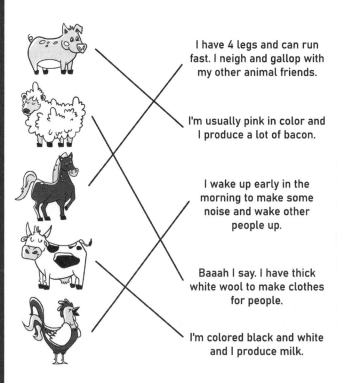

I have 4 legs and can run fast. I neigh and gallop with my other animal friends.

I'm usually pink in color and I produce a lot of bacon.

I wake up early in the morning to make some noise and wake other people up.

Baaah I say. I have thick white wool to make clothes for people.

I'm colored black and white and I produce milk.

66 Farm Stuff

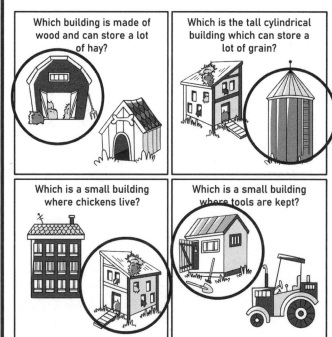

Which building is made of wood and can store a lot of hay?

Which is the tall cylindrical building which can store a lot of grain?

Which is a small building where chickens live?

Which is a small building where tools are kept?

67 Chicken Dance

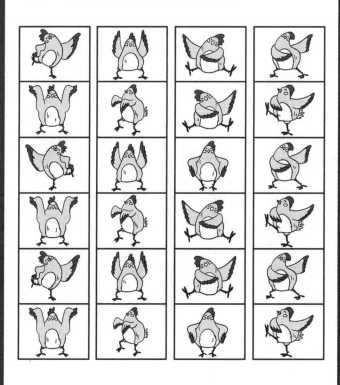

68 Horse Run

88

69 Link the Fences

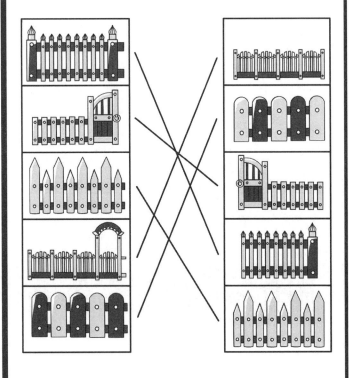

70 Farm Facts

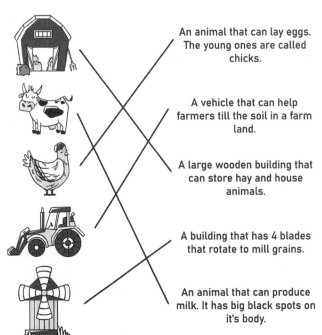

An animal that can lay eggs. The young ones are called chicks.

A vehicle that can help farmers till the soil in a farm land.

A large wooden building that can store hay and house animals.

A building that has 4 blades that rotate to mill grains.

An animal that can produce milk. It has big black spots on it's body.

71 Farm Kids

Emma   Ethan   Mia   Liam   Mason

89

72 Farm Animals

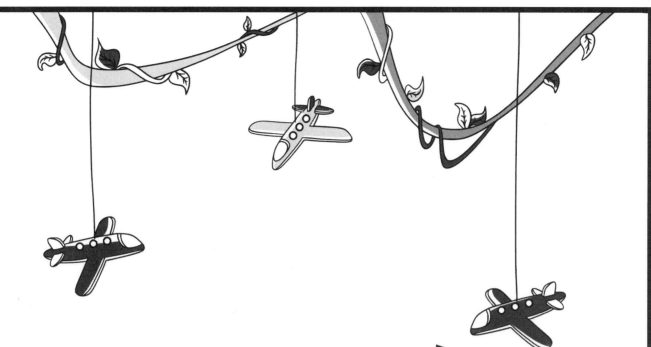

THANK YOU!

We hope you enjoyed the book.
Please consider leaving a review
where you bought it!

For more, please visit:
activitywizo.com